A BEGINNER'S
TO STARTING AN
ONLINE BAKING
BUSINESS

From Home baked Recipes to E-Commerce

Solutions: A Step-by-Step Guide to Starting Your

Own Successful Online Baking Business

KAYLA FLORENCE

TABLE OF CONTENTS

FREE STOCK IMAGES

Pick up your pen and paper to take down important notes as you read this book and get ready to start implementing the moment you are done.

So, let's get started! Grab a cup of coffee and settle in for a journey into the world of online baking. With this guide, you will soon be on your way to success!

Send in any questions you have along the way to **kaylaflores23@gmail.com**

INTRODUCTION

It was a dream come true for Sarah, a young ambitious baker who had always wanted to start her own business. She had spent years perfecting her recipes and perfecting her baking skills and now she was finally ready to take the plunge.

Sarah had always been passionate about baking and had been dreaming of starting her own online baking business since she was a young girl. After months of preparation and hard work, she finally created her own website and was ready to start selling her baked goods.

But she quickly realized that starting an online baking business was more complicated than she had anticipated. There were many things to consider, including finding suppliers, setting up shipping and fulfillment, marketing her business, creating a website, and dealing with customer service.

This book will provide an inside look into the art of starting an online baking business. You will learn the key steps necessary to launch a successful venture, from finding the right suppliers to designing a website and getting your first customers.

With the tips, advice, and stories shared in this book, you will be able to start your own online baking business and make your dreams a reality. The sweet smell of success is something that many aspire to. Baking has long been a way to bring joy to others, and now you can make it your business.

Starting an online baking business can be overwhelming, but with the right guidance and support, you can make it a reality.

This book is all about turning your dream of starting an online baking business into a reality. It will guide you through each step of the process, from deciding on a business model to marketing your products.

You'll learn the ins and outs of pricing, packaging, shipping and more. You'll also get tips on how to maximize profits and grow your business.

You'll also get exclusive recipes and advice from experienced bakers who have already achieved success in their own online businesses. These recipes and advice are designed to help make your business a success.

No matter what your experience level is, this book will provide you with a roadmap for success. So take a deep breath, and let's get started on your journey to becoming an online baking business owner.

INTRODUCTION TO ONLINE BAKING BUSINESS?

Online baking business is a rapidly growing industry in the food and beverage sector. It offers a convenient and cost-effective way for customers to purchase baked goods without having to leave their home.

With the rise of technology, many people are turning to online baking businesses to satisfy their sweet tooth. The online baking business requires a lower start-up cost than a traditional bakery and can be run from anywhere.

The main advantages of an online baking business are the ability to reach a wider customer base, the ability to offer a variety of products, and the convenience of ordering and delivering products quickly.

Online baking businesses have many advantages over traditional bakeries, including access to a wider range of customers.

With an online baking business, you can reach customers who don't live near a traditional bakery and those who would prefer to purchase their baked goods online.

Additionally, you can offer a variety of products, such as custom cakes and cupcakes, to appeal to a larger customer base. You can also offer delivery services, which further increases the convenience of ordering and receiving products.

In order to succeed in an online baking business, it is important to have a comprehensive business plan, a strong online presence, and good customer service. You also need to be knowledgeable about the products that you offer and how to bake them, as well as how to package and ship them.

Additionally, you need to be aware of the regulations related to food safety and labeling. Finally, it is important to be aware of the competition in the industry and to differentiate your business from them.

With the right business plan, a good online presence, and excellent customer service, you can create a successful online baking business. By offering a variety of products, reaching a wider customer base, and providing convenient delivery services, you can quickly build a loyal customer base and start to see profits in your business.

BENEFITS OF STARTING AN ONLINE BAKING BUSINESS

Starting an online baking business can be a great way to make money from home while doing something you love. Not only can you make a living from baking, you can also have the freedom to create whatever treats you like and have customers enjoy them from the comfort of their own homes.

Here are a few of the benefits of starting an online baking business:

1. Low Cost Start-up: Starting an online baking business requires minimal upfront costs. You do not need to invest in expensive equipment or a storefront. All you need is an oven, a few basic ingredients, and an online platform to market and sell your products.

2. Flexible Schedule: Running an online baking business offers you the freedom to set your own hours and work when it is convenient for you. You can take orders online or via phone and fulfill them on your own schedule.

3. Increased Reach: An online baking business can reach a much wider audience than a brick-and-mortar shop. With the right marketing strategy, you can tap into a global market and reach customers all over the world.

4. Unlimited Potential: The sky's the limit when it comes to potential profits from an online baking business. As your business grows, you can add more products, hire staff, and expand your customer base.

Starting an online baking business can be an exciting and rewarding venture. With the right ingredients and a little hard work, you could soon be baking your way to success

CHAPTER 1: GETTING STARTED WITH YOUR ONLINE BAKING BUSINESS

1. Research Your Market: Before you start an online baking business, it's important to understand the local market and what your competition looks like. Research the demographics of your target customers, and consider the pricing and quality of other bakeries in the area.

2. Create a Business Plan: Before launching your online baking business, it's important to create a business plan. This document should include your mission statement, a budget, a marketing plan, and a description of the products or services you'll offer.

3. Choose Your Business Structure: Next, you'll need to decide on the legal structure of your business. Depending on your goals and the size of your business, you may want

to form a corporation, limited liability company, or sole proprietorship.

4. Obtain Necessary Licenses and Permits: Before you can launch your online baking business, you'll need to obtain any necessary business licenses and permits. You may also need to register your business name with the state.

5. Set Up Your Website: The next step is to set up your website. You'll need to choose a domain name, design the layout, and create content that will attract customers. You may also want to invest in an online shopping cart so customers can purchase your baked goods online.

6. Find Wholesale Suppliers: Once your website is up and running, you'll need to find wholesale suppliers for ingredients and other materials. Research local suppliers, and compare prices to find the best deals.

7. Market Your Business: Last but not least, you'll need to market your business. Create a social media presence and consider other digital marketing strategies like SEO, email marketing, and content marketing. You may also want to invest in traditional advertising, like print, radio, and television.

By following these steps, you can get your online baking business off the ground and start selling your products. With the right marketing strategies and a bit of dedication, you can build a successful business.

DISCOVERING YOUR NICHE

1. Research the current trends in the online baking industry. Take some time to explore various websites and blogs related to this field, and read up on what's popular and what's not. This will help you gain insight into the industry, and may even provide you with ideas for your own niche.

2. Determine what sets you apart from other online bakers. Ask yourself "What can I offer that others cannot?". Consider your unique skills, talents, and experiences. Do you have a special talent or interest related to baking? If so, you may have found your niche.

3. Figure out what type of customer you want to target. Think about who your ideal customer is. What do they need? Knowing who you want to serve will help you focus your niche and create content that resonates with your target audience.

4. Brainstorm ideas for your niche. Once you have an idea of what you want to do, write down everything that comes to mind. Don't be afraid to get creative and think outside the box.

5. Test out your niche. Once you have a few ideas, try them out. Test different approaches and see what your target audience enjoys more. This will help you narrow down

your niche and ensure that you're creating content that your customers will love.

By researching the current trends in the online baking industry, determining what sets you apart from other online bakers, figuring out who your ideal customer is, brainstorming ideas for your niche, and testing out different approaches, you can discover your niche in the online baking industry.

HERE'S A LIST OF 40 NICHES IN THE ONLINE BAKING INDUSTRY:

1. Cakes

2. Cupcakes

3. Custom cakes

4. Brownies

5. Muffins

6. Cake Decorating

7. Sugar Cookies

8. Gluten-Free Baking

9. Macarons

10. Vegan Baking

11. Breads

12. Donuts

13. Cupcake Decorating

14. Ice Cream Cakes

15. Pies

16. Cake Pops

17. Wedding Cakes

18. Cheesecakes

19. Chocolate-Making

20. Pastries

21. Candy-Making

22. Special Occasion Cakes

23. Cake Toppers

24. Cake Delivery Services

25. Cookie Decorating

26. Gourmet Cupcakes

27. Biscuits

28. Cake Boards

29. Cake Mixes

30. Cake Drums

31. Fondant Decorating

32. Cake Tins

33. Cake Stands

34. Cake Bags

35. Edible Glitter

36. Cake Tools

37. Cake Wrappers

38. Cake Boxes

39. Cake Flour

40. Cake Fillings

AND HERE'S A LIST OF 20 SPECIAL NICHES IN THE ONLINE BAKING INDUSTRY

1. Organic Baked Goods

2. Gluten-Free Baked Goods

3. Cake Decorating Supplies

4. Keto Baked Goods

5. Vegan Baked Goods

6. Baking Classes

7. Customized Cakes

8. Artisanal Baked Goods

9. Baked Goods Subscription Boxes

10. Baking Tools and Accessories

11. Cupcakes

12. Old-Fashioned Baked Goods

13. Ethnic Baked Goods

14. Customized Baked Goods

15. Baking Mixes

16. Baking for Special Occasions

17. Bakery Gift Boxes

18. Baked Goods for Holidays

19. Baked Goods for Corporate Events

20. Baked Goods for Weddings

CREATING A BUSINESS PLAN

Creating a business plan for an online baking business is an essential step in launching a successful venture. The plan should provide a comprehensive overview of the business, including its mission, objectives, strategies, and financial projections.

The first step in creating a business plan is to define the company's mission. The mission should describe the core purpose of the business, including its goals and objectives. It should also provide a brief overview of the services the business will provide and how it will differentiate itself from the competition.

The next step is to create an outline of the business's strategies. This should include an overview of the competitive landscape and the strategies the business will use to gain an advantage over its competitors. This could include strategies such as offering competitive pricing, providing exceptional customer service, or leveraging discounts and loyalty programs.

GAINING FINANCIAL SUPPORT

When launching an online baking business, gaining financial support is an important part of the process. Here are some strategies to consider:

1. Seek out investors: Reach out to investors and venture capitalists who may be interested in your business. With their financial backing, you can start up your business and expand as needed.

2. Apply for grants: Research local, state, and federal grants that may be available to small businesses. These grants can provide crucial financial support for your business.

3. Utilize crowdfunding platforms: Crowdfunding platforms are an excellent way to gain financial support. Reach out to your network and share your business vision. With their help, you can raise funds to get your business off the ground.

4. Apply for loans: Explore traditional and alternative loan options. Consider applying for a business loan or line of credit to help fund your business.

By following these strategies, you can secure the financial support you need to launch your online baking business.

CHAPTER 2: BUILDING A PROFESSIONAL WEBSITE

1. Brainstorm a Website Design: The first step in creating a professional website for an online baking business is to brainstorm a design that best fits the target audience and the brand identity. This includes selecting a colour palette, font style, and any other design elements that are important to the business.

Some examples of colour palette for the baking industry are:

i.   Misty Rose and Ivory: This colour palette is perfect for a romantic, elegant bakery website. Use a light pink and white combination for a light and airy, yet sophisticated look.

ii. Blueberry and Vanilla: A softer, more casual colour palette, this combination of blue and white is perfect for a bakery website that wants to appear inviting and approachable.

iii. Chocolate and Caramel: This classic combination of brown and yellow is perfect for a bakery website that wants to appear warm and inviting.

2. Set Up a Domain: The next step is to set up a domain for the website. Choosing a domain name that is easy to remember and relevant to the business is important. This website address will be used for all marketing and advertising efforts.

3. Select a Hosting Provider: Selecting a hosting provider is the next step in building a professional website. A hosting provider will provide the servers and infrastructure necessary to support the website and keep it running smoothly.

4. Create Content: Content is the backbone of any website. Creating content for the website should be based on the target audience and the type of products and services the business offers.

Content should be engaging and informative, while also including keywords that are related to the business. Content should also include product descriptions, recipes, photographs of baked goods, customer reviews, contact information, and any other relevant information.

5. Design the Website: After the content is created, the website can be designed. This includes creating the website layout, adding images, and any other design elements that will make the website look professional. Finally, use a

content management system (CMS) to create and manage your content. This will allow you to easily update and edit your website as needed.

6. Launch the Website: The last step is to launch the website. This includes testing the website to make sure it is working correctly and updating any content or design elements that need to be changed. Once the website is launched, it is important to monitor it regularly to make sure it is running smoothly and that all content is up-to-date.

CHOOSING A DOMAIN NAME

When choosing a domain name for an online baking business, it is important to make sure that it is easy to remember, relevant to the business, and available. The domain name should be short and catchy, since this will make it easier for customers to remember. Additionally, it should include relevant keywords that relate to the baking business, such as "bakery" or "cakes".

It is also important to make sure that the domain name is available to register and that it is not already taken by another business. The best way to do this is to search the internet for the domain name in question and see if any other businesses have already registered it. If the domain name is available, then it is important to quickly register it before someone else does.

SELECTING A WEB HOST

Selecting a web host is another important step when building a professional website for an online baking business. When choosing a web host, it is important to ensure that the host is reliable and offers good uptime and customer support.

It is also essential to make sure that the hosting plan is compatible with the type of website that will be built. For example, if the website will be using a content management system (CMS) such as WordPress, then it is important to make sure that the hosting plan supports the CMS.

Once the domain name and web host have been selected, the next step is to design the website.

DESIGNING YOUR WEBSITE

This can be done by using a website builder or by hiring a professional web designer. It is important to make sure that the website design is professional and reflects the brand of the online baking business.

Additionally, the website should be optimized for mobile devices and should be easy to navigate and provide visitor with information they are looking for.

Once the domain name and web host have been selected, the next step is to design the website. This can be done by using a website builder or by hiring a professional web designer.

It is important to make sure that the website design is professional and reflects the brand of the online baking business. Additionally, the website should be optimized for mobile devices and should be easy to navigate.

Finally, the website should be optimized for search engines. This can be done by creating content that is relevant to the business and by optimizing the website's code and structure. This will help to ensure that the website is visible in search engine results when people are searching for online baking businesses.

By following these steps, it is possible to build a professional website for an online baking business. This will help to ensure that the business has a strong presence online and can reach potential customers.

CHAPTER 3: CREATING YOUR BAKING BRAND

When starting an online baking business, it's important to create a unique brand that sets your business apart from the competition. Your brand should be a reflection of your products, values, and the overall mission of your business. Here are a few tips to help you create a memorable baking brand:

1. Define Your Brand's Values: What values do you want your business to represent? This could include qualities like sustainability, quality, or even fun and creativity. Once you have a list of values, you can use them to inform other aspects of your brand.

2. Create a Logo: A memorable logo is an essential part of creating a successful brand. Start by sketching out a few ideas, and then look for a designer who can help you create a polished logo that reflects your values and mission.

3. Develop a Tagline: A tagline should be short and catchy, but also reflect your brand's values. It should be something that resonates with your target audience and helps them remember your business.

4. Establish a Social Media Presence: Social media is an important part of marketing your business and engaging with your customers. Choose a few social media platforms that make sense for your business,

5. Develop a Brand Story: Tell customers about your business and why you're passionate about baking. A compelling story will help customers connect with your brand on an emotional level.

Creating a strong baking brand is an important step when starting an online baking business. With a memorable name, logo, tagline, and story, your products will stand out from the competition and help you build an engaged customer base.

CHOOSING YOUR LOGO

Your logo is more than just a graphic—it's a visual representation of your business. Choosing the right logo is an important part of creating your baking brand.

Start by researching the logos of other successful baking businesses. Note the colors, shapes, fonts, and other design elements they use. This will give you an idea of what works and what doesn't in the baking industry.

Once you've identified potential design elements, create a list of keywords that reflect your business. This could include words like "fresh," "homemade," "artisanal," and "delicious."

Think about how you can incorporate these words into your logo design. For example, you could use a font that looks handwritten to convey a homemade feel. Or you could use bright colors to evoke a sense of freshness and vibrancy.

Finally, don't forget to consider how your logo will look across different mediums.

Whether it's your website, social media, or print material, your logo should be easily recognizable in any format. Consider different font choices, sizes, and colors that will make your logo stand out, no matter the platform.

Having a clear idea of what you want your business to stand for will help you craft a logo that is both meaningful and memorable.

Choosing a logo for your online baking business is an important part of creating a strong brand.

By following these steps, you can ensure that your logo will be one that your customers will remember and recognize.

Some examples of symbols that can be used in your logo are

-Bakery ovens

-Cakes

-Whisk

-Cookies

-Cupcakes

-Pastries

-Chef hats

-Flour

-Baking Utensils

DEVELOPING YOUR BRAND VOICE

Your brand voice should be consistent throughout your website, social media, and other customer-facing materials. It's a reflection of your company's values, mission, and overall personality.

To create a strong brand voice, start by identifying your target audience. This will help you determine which tone and style of language to use when communicating with them. Think about your audience's interests, values, and goals.

Once you've identified your target audience, consider the following questions:

• What words and phrases will resonate with your customers?

• What unique elements can you include in your messaging?

• How can you make your communication style stand out?

You should also think about the type of content you'll be creating. Will you be writing blog posts, creating videos, or running live events? How can you tailor your brand voice to each medium?

By developing a strong brand voice, you can create an authentic connection with your customers and build trust in your business.

Creating an Online Presence/Setting up Social Media Accounts

I.   Creating an Online Presence

    a.   Choose a domain name: Your domain name should be easy to remember and should reflect the nature of your business as discussed earlier.

    b.   Create a website: Building a website is the most important part of setting up your online baking business. You will need to choose a web hosting provider, create a content management system, and design the website.

c. Establish an online store: You will need to decide which payment methods you will accept, create product pages and descriptions, and set up shipping and handling details.

d. Develop content: Creating content is essential for establishing a presence online. You should write blog posts, create videos, and post pictures on social media.

2. Setting up Social Media Accounts

a. Choose the right platforms: You should choose the social media platforms that are the most relevant to your business. For example, if you are a baker, you may want to focus on Instagram, Pinterest, and Facebook.

b. Create profiles: Once you have chosen the right platforms, you should create profiles for each one. Make sure to include a profile picture, a bio, and a link to your website.

c. Post content: Once you have set up your profiles, you should start posting content. Make sure to post regularly to keep your followers engaged.

d. Engage with followers: It is important to engage with your followers and respond to their comments and questions. This will help to build a relationship with your customers and will increase your visibility online.

e. Monitor analytics: Tracking the performance of your social media accounts will help you to understand what content works and what doesn't. Make sure to monitor your analytics regularly to keep track of your progress.

CHAPTER 4. FINDING SUPPLIES AND INGREDIENTS

The success of an online baking business depends on finding the right supplies and ingredients to produce high-quality products. Quality ingredients are essential to

When searching for supplies, it is important to consider factors such as freshness, cost, and variety.Finding supplies and ingredients is an essential step for starting an online baking business. You will need to source ingredients and supplies in order to create your products.

Do the following when Finding Supplies and Ingredients:

1. Research local suppliers and wholesalers of baking ingredients and supplies. Take time to compare prices and find the best deals.

2. Consider purchasing in bulk to save money on ingredients.

3. Look into online vendors for specialty ingredients and supplies.

4. Take advantage of seasonal sales and discounts to stock up on supplies.

5. Compare shipping costs and delivery times when shopping online.

6. Look for coupons and promo codes to save money on purchases.

7. Consider investing in quality baking tools and equipment for better results.

A. WHERE TO BUY INGREDIENTS

1. Research local businesses that sell baking ingredients. Look for stores that specialize in baking supplies and have a good reputation. Ask friends and family for recommendations.

2. Search online for baking suppliers. Many companies sell baking ingredients and supplies on the Internet. Look for companies that offer competitive prices and reliable shipping times.

3. Compare prices and shipping times for different companies. Choose the vendor that offers the best deal for your needs.

4. Contact local farmers and producers to inquire about purchasing ingredients. This is a great way to get fresh, high-quality ingredients.

5. Consider buying in bulk from a wholesale club or online wholesale store. This can be a great way to save money if you plan on using a lot of the same ingredients.

B. FINDING THE RIGHT SUPPLIES AND EQUIPMENTS

The right supplies can make or break a product, so it is important to choose the right ones.

When finding supplies, start by researching the different types of supplies that are available. Consider the different types of baking tools, such as baking pans, measuring cups, mixers, spatulas, and whisks.

Also research the different types of ingredients available, including flour, sugar, butter, eggs, and other baking staples. Take time to look at the different brands and prices of each item to find the best deals.

Also consider the packaging for your products. Research the different types of packaging available, such as boxes, bags, wrappers, and labels. Consider the cost of the packaging and the durability of the materials to ensure that your products are securely packaged and protected during shipping.

By taking the time to research the different types of supplies available, you can ensure that you are finding the best products for your online baking business. Quality supplies will make your products stand out and attract customers who will return for more.

C. HOW TO FIND THE RIGHT EQUIPMENTS

The first step in finding the right equipment is to identify what you need. Ask yourself what kind of baking you plan to do. Baking cookies, cakes, bread, and other items all require different tools and equipment. Consider what kinds of products you want to make and how many you plan to make. This will help you determine what equipment you will need.

Once you know what you need, start researching the different types of equipment on the market. Talk to other bakers and research online to see what equipment other bakers use. Look for reviews and ratings of products to make sure you are investing in quality equipment.

Once you have narrowed down your selection, it's time to start shopping. Look for a vendor who can provide you with the equipment you need. Make sure to check the vendor's return policy, warranty, and customer service.

When you have found the right equipment, it's important to take care of it. Clean and sanitize all equipment before and after use. Make sure to follow the manufacturer's instructions for storage and maintenance.

Finding the right equipment for your online baking business is essential for success. Take the time to research, shop around, and invest in quality equipment that will last. With the right equipment, you can create delicious treats to share with your customers.

CHAPTER 5: OFFERING BAKING SERVICES

Starting a home-based online baking business can be both rewarding and fun! With the right tools and recipes, you can create delicious sweet and savory treats for your customers.

From custom cakes and cupcakes to artisan breads and cookies, you can offer a wide variety of services to fit your customers' needs. Let your creativity shine and make your customers' dreams come true with your homemade treats.

You can also choose to offer delivery services to make it easier for your customers to enjoy your delectable confections. other unique services include custom cake toppers, edible images, and cake decorating classes. Let your online baking business take flight!

Developing a Pricing Strategy Developing a pricing strategy for an online baking business is an important part of creating a successful business. It is important to considr the cost of ingredients, overhead costs such as rent and utilities, and the time required to create each item.

Additionally, some customers may be willing to pay a premium for a custom-made item or for special dietary requirements.

It is also important to consider the competition, as pricing should not be so high that no one will purchase the products.

Finally, pricing should be consistent and fair, as customers should not be charged more for the same item. By taking all of these factors into consideration, a pricing strategy can be created that will ensure the success of an online baking business.

You can follow the format below when fixing prices for the services you offer

• Basic-level services: These are entry-level services that provide basic baked goods such as cookies, muffins, and cupcakes. Prices for these services can range from $10 to $20 per item.

• Specialty services: These are services that offer more customized baked goods such as wedding cakes and other specialty items. Prices for these services can range from $30 to $50 per item.

• Premium services: These are services that offer top-of-the-line baked goods such as multi-tiered cakes and other specialty items. Prices for these services can range from $50 to $100 per item.

The following factors should be put into consideration when fixing prices for the services you offer. Although stated above, they are outlined here for easy comprehension

• Cost of ingredients: This should be factored into each item's price in order to ensure that the cost of ingredients is being covered and that a profit is being earned.

• Overhead costs: These costs should be factored into the pricing structure in order to ensure that the business is profitable.

• Time required: The amount of time required to create each item should be considered when setting prices in order to ensure that the business is earning a profit.

• Competition: Prices should be competitive with what other bakers are charging in order to ensure that customers are willing to purchase the items.

• Consistency: Prices should be consistent in order to ensure that customers are not charged more for the same item.

• Special requests: Customers may be willing to pay a premium for custom-made items or special dietary requirements, so this should be taken into account when setting prices.

CREATING A MENU

Creating a menu for an online baking business is an important step in creating a successful business. Here are some tips to help you create a menu that will attract customers and keep them coming back:

1. Identify Your Target Audience: Determine who your target customers are and what their needs and wants are. This will help you decide which types of baked goods to include on your menu.

2. Research Popular Baked Goods: Based on the preferences of your target audience, research popular baked goods to determine which items you should include on your menu.

3. Offer Variety: Offer a variety of baked goods to appeal to a wide range of customers. Consider offering different flavors, sizes, and styles to cater to different tastes.

4. Keep It Simple: Avoid having too many items on your menu. Having too many items can be overwhelming and make it difficult for customers to decide which items to choose.

5. Highlight Specialties: Highlight your specialties and unique items on your menu to draw customers in.

6. Incorporate Seasonal Items: Incorporate seasonal items into your menu to keep customers interested. Offer items such as pumpkin spice cupcakes, eggnog cookies, or peppermint brownies during the holidays.

7. Promote Healthy Options: Offer healthier options such as vegan, gluten-free, or low-sugar items to cater to customers with special dietary needs.

8. Update Your Menu Regularly: Keep your menu fresh and interesting by updating it regularly. Try introducing new items or special offers to keep customers coming back.

Creating a menu for your online baking business is an important step in ensuring the success of your business. With the right menu, you can attract customers and keep them coming back for more!

The following components should be included in your menu

• A list of all the bakery items you offer

• The price of each item

• Descriptions of each item

• Nutritional information (if available)

• Photos or illustrations of each item

• Special offers or promotions

• Seasonal items

• Healthy options

• Delivery or pick-up information

- Contact information

- Terms and conditions

- Payment methods accepted

DEVELOPING DELIVERY AND PICKUP OPTIONS

it is important to develop delivery and pickup options for customers. Delivery allows customers to have their orders sent directly to their home or office, while pickup allows customers to pick up their orders from a designated location.

DELIVERY

When developing delivery options for an online baking business, it is important to consider the type of delivery service that best fits the business's needs. For example, a business may choose to use a third-party delivery service such as UPS or FedEx, or they may decide to use their own delivery service. It is also important to consider the cost of delivery, as well as the customer's satisfaction with the delivery service.

PICKUP

Pickup options can be a convenient way for customers to receive their orders. When developing pickup options, it is important to consider the location of the pickup point, as well as the hours of operation.

A business may choose to have customers pick up their orders from their shop, or they may choose to designate a nearby location as the pickup point. It is also important to consider the customer's satisfaction with the pickup process, and to ensure that customers have a positive experience.

No matter what delivery and pickup options a business chooses to offer, it is important to ensure that customers are provided with a seamless experience. When developing delivery and pickup options for an online baking business, it is important to ensure that the options are convenient, reliable, and cost-effective.

CHAPTER 6: HOW TO CREATE A RANGE OF DELICIOUS BAKED GOODS

1. Research and Select Recipes: Before you start your online baking business, it is important to research and select recipes that you feel confident baking and that you know will be successful.

Look for recipes that are easy to make, use ingredients that are readily available, and that create a delicious final product.

2. Test Your Recipes: Once you have selected your recipes, it is important to test them out. This will help you make sure that the recipes are reliable and that you can confidently bake them for your customers.

3. Gather Necessary Supplies: You will need to make sure that you have all of the necessary supplies for baking your recipes. Gather all of the ingredients, baking pans, and any other equipment you will need.

4. Create Packaging: You will need to create packaging for your baked goods. This could include boxes, bags, labels, and more. Make sure that the packaging looks professional and reflects the quality of your product.

1.1 EQUIPMENT AND INGREDIENTS

Equipment:

If you're planning to start an online baking business, there are certain pieces of equipment you will need. These include ovens, pans, baking tools, a mixer, a refrigerator, and a large workspace. You'll also need measuring cups, spoons, and other utensils.

Ingredients:

The ingredients you'll need to start your online baking business will depend on the type of baking you plan to do. Common ingredients include flour, sugar, butter, eggs, baking powder, baking soda, and other items. You'll also need to purchase specialty ingredients such as chocolate, nuts, and dried fruits. Additionally, you may need to purchase food coloring, extracts, and other additives.

1.2 TECHNIQUES FOR MAKING DELICIOUS BAKED GOODS

: 1. Invest in quality ingredients. Using the freshest, highest-quality ingredients will make your baked goods stand out from the rest.

2. Perfect your recipes. Make sure you have a tried-and-true recipe that you are confident in. Practice makes perfect!

3. Pay attention to detail. Make sure that you measure carefully and follow the directions precisely.

4. Use the right equipment. Invest in the right tools and equipment, such as a good set of measuring cups, mixing bowls, and baking pans.

5. Preheat your oven. Make sure your oven is preheated to the temperature called for in the recipe before you begin baking.

6. Don't overmix. Overmixing can make baked goods dense and tough, so be careful not to overdo it.

7. Use correct baking times. Set a timer to ensure that your baked goods are not over-baked or under-baked.

8. Cool properly. Allow your baked goods to cool completely before packaging or serving.

2. CAKES

Cakes are a type of sweet dessert that is typically made with flour, sugar, eggs, butter, and various flavorings such as vanilla, chocolate, or fruit.

Cakes can be decorated with frosting, fruits, nuts, chocolate chips, and other edible decorations. Some popular cake flavors include vanilla, chocolate, red velvet, lemon, carrot, and banana.

Cakes can be served as a dessert, as a snack, or as a special occasion cake. They can be baked in a variety of shapes such as round, square, or heart-shaped.

Cakes can also be made with or without frosting or other toppings. Popular cake flavors for special occasions include wedding cakes, birthday cakes, and holiday cakes.

2.1 Types of Cakes

Cakes are a staple of special occasions and celebrations. From birthdays to weddings and showers to anniversaries, cakes bring people together to enjoy a delicious treat.

There are many different types of cakes, with a variety of flavors, toppings, and fillings. From light and airy angel food cake to decadent chocolate fudge cake, there is something for everyone to enjoy. Some of the most popular types of cakes include:

Chiffon Cake: Chiffon cake is a light, airy cake made with oil instead of butter, making it a great choice for those who are looking for a lighter cake option. It is often flavored with lemon or orange, and it can be served with a variety of toppings, like fruit or whipped cream.

Cheesecake: Cheesecake is one of the most popular types of cakes. It is made with a creamy filling and can be topped with a variety of different flavors. Traditional flavors include cherry, strawberry, and blueberry.

Red Velvet Cake: Red velvet cake is a classic cake that is perfect for special occasions. It is made with cocoa powder, buttermilk, and red food coloring, giving it a unique flavor and color.

Carrot Cake: Carrot cake is a moist cake that is filled with carrots, nuts, and spices. It is usually topped with a cream cheese frosting and is a popular choice for birthdays and other special occasions.

Angel Food Cake: Angel food cake is a light and airy cake that is made with egg whites and no butter. It is often served with fresh fruit and whipped cream.

Pound Cake: Pound cake is a dense, buttery cake that is typically flavoured with vanilla or almond extract. It is often served with a glaze or frosting, and it can be served in many different shapes, like a loaf or a bundt cake.

Fruit Cake: Fruit cake is a dense cake that is filled with dried and candied fruits. It is often served during the holidays and is usually topped with a brandy or rum glaze.

Chocolate Cake: Chocolate cake is a classic cake that is perfect for any occasion. It can be topped with a variety of different frostings and fillings, like chocolate mousse or ganache.

Cupcakes: Cupcakes are a fun, bite-sized version of cakes that are perfect for parties or special occasions. They can come in a variety of flavors, like vanilla, chocolate, and red velvet, and they can be topped with a variety of different frostings.

Ice Cream Cake: Ice cream cake is a fun and unique way to enjoy cake. It is made with layers of ice cream and cake, and it is often topped with frosting and sprinkles.

Banana Cake: Banana cake is a moist cake that is made with mashed bananas and often topped with cream cheese frosting. It is a great option for those who are looking for a unique and delicious cake.

These are just some of the most popular types of cakes.

There are many more varieties to choose from that are sure to please any crowd. Whether your potential customers are looking for something light and airy or rich and decadent, there is a cake that is perfect for any occasion.

2.2 How to Make Moist and Fluffy Cakes

Cakes are the desserts of choice for many special occasions, from anniversaries and birthdays to holidays and weddings.

To ensure that your special occasion is extra special, it's important to make sure your cake is moist and fluffy.

Below are some tips for making moist and fluffy cakes that will be sure to wow your guests.

1. Use the Correct Batter Consistency – Make sure your batter is thick enough to hold its shape when scooped, yet thin enough to spread easily. Too much liquid in the batter will cause the cake to be dense and heavy.

2. Measure Ingredients Accurately – To ensure your cake is moist and fluffy, it's important to measure your ingredients accurately. Too much of an ingredient can make the cake tough and dry.

3. Use Room Temperature Ingredients – Room temperature ingredients mix more evenly and help create a moist cake.

4. Beat the Batter Well – Be sure to beat the batter until everything is well-combined. This will help incorporate air into the batter, which will create a fluffier cake.

5. Bake at the Right Temperature – Baking at the right temperature will help ensure your cake is moist and fluffy. Too low of a temperature and the cake won't bake properly, and too high of a temperature will dry out the cake.

6. Check for Doneness – As soon as a toothpick inserted into the center of the cake comes out clean, it's time to take it out of the oven.

7. Cool the Cake Properly – Cooling the cake properly will help keep it from drying out. Let the cake cool in the pan for 10 to 15 minutes before turning it out onto a cooling rack.

Following these tips will help ensure that your cakes are moist and fluffy.

2.3 Tips for Decorating Cakes

The art of cake decorating is an age-old tradition that has been passed down from generation to generation. With a few simple tips and tricks, anyone can create beautiful, unique cakes for any special occasion.

Whether you are just starting an online baking business or you are a seasoned professional, here are some tips for decorating cakes that will help you make your cakes look amazing.

1. Get creative with icing - Icing can be used to create almost any design or pattern. Experiment with different colors and textures to give your cakes a special look.

2. Use fondant to create shapes - Fondant is a great material for creating intricate shapes and designs. It comes in a variety of colors and can be used to make 3D shapes, such as flowers, animals, and even characters.

3. Play with texture - Try adding different textures to your cakes with various ingredients. You can use coconut, nuts, sprinkles, and other toppings to give your cake an interesting look.

4. Be careful with colors - Too many colors can make your cake look garish and unappetizing. Stick to two or three

colors that complement each other and make sure to use a light touch.

5. Use edible decorations - Edible decorations such as sugar flowers, fondant figures, and edible glitter are all great ways to add a unique touch to your cakes.

6. Practice makes perfect - Don't be afraid to practice your decorating skills. With a little practice, you'll be able to create beautiful, unique cakes for your customers.

With these tips for decorating cakes, you'll be able to create stunning cakes that will be sure to impress your customers. So my dear bakers, don't forget to have fun and get creative with your cakes!

3: PIES

Pies are a type of pastry dessert that is typically made with a crust and filled with a sweet or savory filling. Sweet pies may be filled with fruit, nuts, chocolate, or custard.

Savory pies may be filled with meat, seafood, cheese, or vegetables. Pies are some of the most popular desserts in the world and can be found in many different cultures.

Popular pie varieties include apple, blueberry, pumpkin, pecan, and cherry. Pies can also be made with a variety of crusts, such as shortcrust, puff pastry, and graham cracker.

Pies are a great option for an online baking business as they are popular, versatile, and can be customized to fit individual tastes.

Additionally, pies can be easily packaged and shipped, making them an ideal product for an online business.

3.1 Types of Pies

1. Apple Pie: The classic, timeless apple pie is a favorite of many. It is made with a pastry crust filled with a sweetened mixture of tart apples, cinnamon, and sugar.

2. Cherry Pie: This tart and sweet treat is made with a pastry crust and a filling of cherries, sugar, and spices.

3. Key Lime Pie: This creamy pie is made with a graham cracker crust and a tart, custard-like filling made of key limes, condensed milk, and egg yolks.

4. Pecan Pie: This Southern classic is made with a pastry crust and a sweet, gooey filling of pecans, corn syrup, butter, and sugar.

5. Pumpkin Pie: This autumn favorite is made with a pastry crust and a spiced pumpkin filling made of pureed pumpkin, spices, and condensed milk.

6. Blueberry Pie: This classic pie is made with a pastry crust and a sweet, fruity filling of blueberries, lemon juice, and sugar.

7. Peach Pie: This summertime favorite is made with a pastry crust and a sweet filling of peaches, spices, and sugar.

8. Strawberry Rhubarb Pie: This tart and sweet pie is made with a pastry crust and a filling of strawberries, rhubarb, and sugar.

9. Chocolate Cream Pie: This decadent treat is made with a pastry crust and a creamy filling of milk, sugar, cocoa, and eggs.

10. Banana Cream Pie: This classic dessert is made with a pastry crust and a creamy filling of bananas, milk, sugar, and eggs.

3.2 Tips for Making Perfect Pie Crusts

1. Start with quality ingredients: Use a high-quality all-purpose flour and butter that is cold.

2. Cut the butter into small pieces: The goal is to have small pieces of butter distributed throughout the dough.

3. Use cold water: Using cold water helps to make sure the butter doesn't melt too quickly and helps to create a flaky crust.

4. Chill the dough: After mixing together the ingredients, chill the dough for at least 30 minutes before rolling it out.

5. Roll it out on a lightly floured surface: Make sure the surface is lightly floured to prevent sticking.

6. Cut the dough to size: Use a ruler or measuring tape to make sure the dough is the correct size before placing it in the pan.

7. Pre-bake if necessary: Some recipes may require pre-baking the crust before adding the filling.

8. Bake until golden brown: Keep an eye on the crust while it's baking. It should be golden brown when it's done.

9. Let it cool: Let the pie crust cool completely before serving.

3.3 Filling Ideas for Pies

1. Apple Pie – Apples, cinnamon, nutmeg and sugar.

2. Cherry Pie – Fresh cherries, sugar, cornstarch, and butter.

3. Blueberry Pie – Fresh or frozen blueberries, sugar, cornstarch, and butter.

4. Peach Pie – Fresh or frozen peaches, sugar, cornstarch, and butter.

5. Mixed Berry Pie – A combination of blueberries, raspberries, blackberries, and strawberries, sugar, cornstarch, and butter.

6. Pumpkin Pie – Pumpkin puree, sugar, eggs, spices, and evaporated milk.

7. Pecan Pie – Pecans, eggs, butter, sugar, and corn syrup.

8. Chocolate Cream Pie – Chocolate, sugar, eggs, evaporated milk, and butter.

9. Key Lime Pie – Lime juice, sweetened condensed milk, eggs, and butter.

10. Strawberry Rhubarb Pie – Fresh or frozen strawberries, rhubarb, sugar, cornstarch, and butter.

11. Coconut Cream Pie – Coconut milk, sugar, eggs, cornstarch, and butter.

12. Banana Cream Pie – Bananas, sugar, eggs, evaporated milk, and butter.

13. Lemon Meringue Pie – Lemon juice, sugar, eggs, cornstarch, and butter.

14. Chocolate Chip Pie – Chocolate chips, sugar, eggs, evaporated milk, and butter.

15. Caramel Apple Pie – Apples, caramel, sugar, cornstarch, and butter.

4: COOKIES

Cookies are small, flat, sweet treats that are usually made from flour, sugar, butter, eggs, and other ingredients. They are often flavored with vanilla, spices, chocolate chips, and other flavorings. Cookies are commonly baked in an oven and served as a snack or dessert.

4.1 Types of Cookies

1. Chocolate Chip Cookies: Chocolate chip cookies are one of the most popular types of cookies. They are usually made with butter, sugar, eggs, vanilla extract, baking soda, and semi-sweet chocolate chips.

2. Oatmeal Cookies: Oatmeal cookies are made with rolled oats, butter, sugar, eggs, and spices like cinnamon and nutmeg. They can also be made with raisins, nuts, and other dried fruits.

3. Sugar Cookies: Sugar cookies are made with butter, sugar, eggs, vanilla extract, baking powder, and flour. The dough is rolled out and cut into shapes before being baked.

4. Peanut Butter Cookies: Peanut butter cookies are made with butter, sugar, eggs, vanilla extract, baking soda, and peanut butter. They are usually rolled into ball shapes before baking.

5. Shortbread Cookies: Shortbread cookies are made with butter, sugar, eggs, and flour. They are usually made in a round or rectangular shape, and they have a crumbly texture.

6. Snickerdoodles: Snickerdoodles are made with butter, sugar, eggs, vanilla extract, baking soda, and cinnamon. They are rolled into balls before baking and then rolled in a mixture of sugar and cinnamon.

7. Gingersnaps: Gingersnaps are made with butter, sugar, eggs, vanilla extract, baking soda, and ground ginger. They are usually rolled into balls and then flattened before baking.

8. Macaroons: Macaroons are made with shredded coconut, sweetened condensed milk, eggs, and vanilla extract. They are usually shaped into crescents or small balls before baking.

9. Molasses Cookies: Molasses cookies are made with butter, sugar, eggs, molasses, baking soda, and spices like cinnamon and nutmeg. They are usually rolled into balls and flattened before baking.

10. Sandwich Cookies: Sandwich cookies are made with two cookies that are filled with a sweet or savory filling. Popular fillings include buttercream, ganache, or jam.

11. Brownies: Brownies are made with melted chocolate, butter, sugar, eggs, and flour. They have a dense, fudgy texture and can be topped with nuts or chocolate chips.

12. Biscotti: Biscotti are Italian cookies that are made with butter, sugar, eggs, flour, and baking powder. They are shaped into logs and then sliced before baking.

13. Meringues: Meringues are made with egg whites, sugar, and vanilla extract. They are usually made into small, fluffy clouds and they are crispy when they are finished baking.

14. Shortcakes: Shortcakes are made with butter, sugar, eggs, flour, and baking powder. They are usually shaped into round or rectangular shapes before baking and then topped with sweetened whipped cream and fresh fruit.

15. Madeleines: Madeleines are small French cakes that are made with butter, sugar, eggs, flour, and baking powder. They have a unique shell-like shape, and they are usually served with a dusting of powdered sugar.

4.2 Tips for Making Perfect Cookies

1. Use Room Temperature Ingredients – Make sure that all of your ingredients, including butter and eggs, are at room temperature before getting started. This ensures that each ingredient will combine properly, resulting in evenly-baked cookies.

2. Measure Ingredients Accurately – Measure each ingredient carefully and accurately. Use a kitchen scale for dry ingredients and a measuring cup for liquid ingredients.

3. Chill the Dough – Chilling cookie dough before baking helps to prevent spreading and ensure a chewy center.

4. Don't Over-Mix the Dough – Over-mixing the dough will cause the cookies to become tough. Mix just until the ingredients are blended.

5. Use Fresh Baking Soda and Baking Powder – Make sure to use fresh baking soda and baking powder for the best results.

6. Bake at the Proper Temperature – The temperature of your oven can make a big difference in how your cookies turn out. Follow the recipe exactly and use an oven thermometer to ensure accuracy.

7. Don't Over-Bake – Cookies should be removed from the oven when they are slightly under-baked. This will ensure that they are soft and chewy.

8. Allow Cookies to Cool – Allow the cookies to cool completely on the baking sheet before removing them. This helps the cookies to firm up and keeps them from falling apart.

9. Store Properly – Store cookies in an airtight container or zip-top bag. This will keep them fresh and delicious.

4.3 Decorating Ideas for Cookies

Decorating cookies can be a fun and creative activity for bakers of all skill levels. Whether you're making cookies for a special occasion or just for fun, here are a few decorating ideas you can use to turn ordinary cookies into something extra special.

1. Royal Icing: Royal icing is a traditional cookie decorating method that uses a paste made from powdered sugar and egg whites or meringue powder. This icing can be used to pipe intricate designs and details onto cookies, or to create a smooth, glossy finish. It's best for cookies

that don't need to be eaten right away, since royal icing hardens quickly.

2. Sprinkles and Sugars: Sprinkles and sugars are a great way to add color and texture to cookies. You can buy pre-made mixes of sprinkles, or create your own custom mixes. Make sure to use non-melting sugars, such as sanding sugars, for the best results.

3. Chocolate Decorations: Chocolate decorations are a great way to add a special touch to cookies. You can use melted chocolate to create intricate designs and details, or you can use pre-made decorations such as chocolate chips or candy melts.

4. Edible Glitter: Edible glitter is a fun and easy way to add sparkle and shine to cookies. It comes in a variety of colors and sizes and can be used to create a glittery effect.

5. Fondant: Fondant is a type of sugar paste that can be used to create intricate decorations for cookies. It's great for shaping and sculpting, but it does require some practice to master.

6. Paint and Dyes: Paint and food dyes can be used to create colorful and unique decorations for cookies. You can

use edible gold or silver paint to create a metallic effect, or you can use food dyes to create detailed designs.

7. Icing Pens: Icing pens are a great way to quickly add details and designs to cookies. They're easy to use, and they come in a variety of colors.

No matter which decorating method you choose, the cookies would definitely come out nice.

5: BREADS

Breads are baked goods made with flour, yeast, water, and other ingredients such as milk, eggs, butter, sugar, and salt

5.1 Types of Breads

Artisan Breads

Artisan breads are made with traditional methods and recipes, often with natural fermentation. This type of bread is produced using high-quality ingredients and a slow, lengthy process. Artisan breads generally have a unique flavor, texture, and appearance. Examples of artisan breads include sourdough, ciabatta, focaccia, baguettes, and rye breads.

Whole-Grain Breads

Whole-grain breads are made with whole grains instead of refined grains, which means they have more fiber, vitamins, minerals, and protein than white bread. Whole-grain breads can be made with a variety of grains, such as oats, wheat, rye, barley, millet, and quinoa. Examples of whole-grain breads include whole wheat, oat bread, rye bread, and multigrain bread.

Flatbreads

Flatbreads are thin, unleavened breads that can be made with a variety of grains and flours. Examples of flatbreads include naan, pita, tortilla, lavash, and roti. These breads are usually cooked on a hot surface, such as a griddle or skillet, and can be served warm or cold.

Gluten-Free Breads

Gluten-free breads are made without wheat, barley, or rye, which means they do not contain gluten. These breads are often made with alternative flours, such as almond flour, buckwheat flour, or rice flour. Examples of gluten-free breads include almond flour bread, buckwheat bread, and rice flour bread.

Quick Breads

Quick breads are leavened breads that do not require yeast or a lengthy rising process. These breads are usually made with baking soda or baking powder as a leavening agent. Examples of quick breads include banana bread, cornbread, and zucchini bread.

Sourdough Breads

Sourdough breads are made with a sourdough starter, which is a combination of flour and water that has been fermented with wild yeast. Sourdough breads have a unique, tangy flavor and a chewy texture. Examples of sourdough breads include San Francisco sourdough, rye sourdough, and whole wheat sourdough.

No-Knead Breads

No-knead breads are made without kneading the dough, which makes them easy to prepare. These breads usually require a long fermentation process, which helps to develop flavoand texture.

Examples of no-knead breads include honey oat bread, sourdough bread, and whole wheat bread.

Fruit & Nut Breads

Fruit and nut breads are made with a variety of dried fruits and nuts. These breads are usually sweet, and can be served as a snack or dessert. Examples of fruit and nut breads include cranberry walnut bread, banana nut bread, and date nut bread.

Brioche

Brioche is a rich, buttery bread that is made with eggs and butter. This type of bread is usually sweet, and is often served as a dessert or breakfast item. Brioche can be made into dinner rolls, loaves, or even shaped into a sweet loaf.

Specialty Breads

Specialty breads are unique breads that are made with a variety of ingredients, such as herbs, spices, fruits, nuts, and cheeses. These breads can be savory or sweet, and can be served as an appetizer, side dish, or even a main course. Examples of specialty breads include focaccia, rosemary olive oil bread, and cheesy garlic bread.

Ciabatta

Ciabatta is an Italian white bread that is made with a wet dough. This type of bread has a crisp crust and a soft, airy texture. Ciabatta can be served as a sandwich bread, or as an accompaniment to soup or salad.

English Muffins

English muffins are a type of yeast-leavened bread that is cooked on a griddle or skillet. These muffins are usually smaller than regular bread, and have a chewy texture. English muffins can be served with butter and jam, or used as a sandwich base.

Bagels

Bagels are a type of bread that is boiled and then baked. Bagels are usually made with wheat flour, and are shaped into a circular shape. They can be served plain, or topped with a variety of toppings, such as sesame seeds, poppy seeds, or dried onions.

Baguettes

Baguettes are a type of French bread that is made with a lean dough and a long, thin shape. These breads have a crisp crust and a light, airy texture. Baguettes can be served as a sandwich bread, or as an accompaniment to soup or salad.

Focaccia

Focaccia is an Italian flatbread that is made with olive oil, herbs, and salt. This type of bread is usually topped with a variety of toppings, such as olives, tomatoes, and onions. Focaccia can be served as a side dish, or as an appetizer.

5.2 Techniques for Making Delicious Breads

1. Start with Quality Ingredients: Start by selecting quality ingredients for your recipes. Look for organic and unbleached flour, fresh yeast, and natural sweeteners. Selecting quality ingredients will help ensure that your breads are delicious.

2. Knead Properly: Kneading is the process of folding, stretching, and compressing dough. Proper kneading helps to create an ideal texture and flavor in your breads.

3. Allow Adequate Rising Time: Allowing your bread dough to rise gives it time to develop flavor and texture. Make sure you allow adequate time for the dough to rise before baking.

4. Use the Right Pan: Using the right type of pan can make a big difference in the quality of your breads. Use a heavy-duty pan with a lid to help keep the bread's shape and keep it moist.

5. Use the Right Temperature: Baking temperature is important for getting the best results from your breads. Always preheat your oven and use a thermometer to check the temperature before baking.

6. Monitor the Baking Time: Baking time will vary depending on the type of bread you are baking. Use a timer and keep an eye on the bread as it bakes.

7. Cool and Store Properly: Allow your breads to cool completely before storing. Wrap in plastic wrap or place in an airtight container to prevent them from drying out.

8. Experiment: Once you've mastered the basics, don't be afraid to experiment. Try adding different ingredients and flavors to create unique and delicious breads.

9. Enjoy: Most of all, don't forget to enjoy the process of baking and the delicious results

.

5.3 Toppings and Fillings for Breads

1. Cinnamon and Sugar

2. Chocolate Chips

3. Sliced Almonds

4. Cranberries

5. Chopped Walnuts

6. Dates

7. Raisins

8. Apricots

9. Figs

10. Sunflower Seeds

11. Pecans

12. Marshmallows

13. Cream Cheese

14. Nutella

15. Peanut Butter

16. Caramel

17. Apple Pie Filling

18. Banana

19. Jam or Jelly

20. Brown Sugar

21. Olive Oil

22. Coconut

23. Butterscotch

24. Honey

25. White Chocolate Chips

6: FINISHING TOUCHES

Finishing Touches to your Baked Goods

1. Glazing and Icing – A beautiful glaze or icing is the perfect way to add extra sweetness and color to your baked goods. Try mixing different colors of icing or experimenting with different flavors.

2. Sprinkles and Toppings – Sprinkles, chopped nuts, and candy are all great toppings to add extra flavor and texture to your baked goods.

3. Fondant – Fondant is a type of icing that can be used to create fun shapes and decorations. It is also great for covering cakes and cupcakes.

4. Chocolate Drizzle – A chocolate drizzle is a great way to add an extra bit of chocolate to your baked goods.

5. Edible Flowers – Edible flowers are a beautiful and unique way to add a touch of elegance to your baked goods.

6. Sea Salt – Sprinkling a bit of sea salt on top of your baked goods will add a delicious salty flavor.

7. Fruit – Fresh or dried fruit can be used to add a bit of sweetness and color to your baked goods.

8. Nuts – Chopped nuts are a great way to add an extra bit of crunch and flavor to your baked goods.

9. Jam – Jam is a great way to add an extra bit of sweetness and color to your baked goods.

10. Powdered Sugar – Powdered sugar is a beautiful and tasty way to finish off your baked goods.

6.1 Ideas for Presentation of your baked goods online

1. Create a visually appealing website that showcases your products. Use high-quality images, videos, and descriptions of your baked goods to make them more appealing to potential customers.

2. Showcase customer reviews and ratings on your website to encourage potential customers to purchase your products.

3. Create a blog for your baking business and post recipes, tips, and stories about your baking journey.

4. Host live baking sessions on your website or social media accounts and encourage customers to join in and bake along with you.

5. Use online advertising platforms such as Google Ads, Facebook Ads, and Instagram Ads to reach a wider audience.

6. Create an email list and send out offers and promotions to your subscribers.

7. Offer discounts or free samples to encourage customers to purchase your products.

8. Participate in online forums, Facebook groups, and other discussion communities related to baking and food to build an online presence.

9. Develop a presence on social media platforms such as Instagram, Facebook, and Twitter, and use them to post updates and answer customer inquiries.

10. Partner with influencers in the food industry and ask them to review your products.

11. Reach out to food bloggers and ask them to write a review or feature your products on their blog.

12. Create an online baking course and offer it to customers who purchase your products.

13. Host giveaways and competitions on your website or social media accounts to increase engagement with potential customers.

14. Create an affiliate program and offer commission to affiliates who promote and sell your products.

15. Use virtual reality and augmented reality technologies to create an immersive experience for your customers.

6.2 Tips for Storing Baked Goods

1. Store all baked goods in airtight containers or wrap them in plastic wrap. This will help keep the items fresh and free from humidity.

2. Place items in a cool, dry place. A pantry or kitchen cabinet works well, though you may need to check the temperature of the space you're storing in from time to time.

3. Label all items and date them when you store them so you can keep track of when you made them.

4. If you are baking items with nuts, it is best to store them in the refrigerator or freezer as the oils in nuts can cause them to go bad quickly.

5. Store cakes, muffins, and cupcakes in the refrigerator if they are not being eaten within a few days. This will help keep them from spoiling.

6. If you are freezing items, let them cool completely before wrapping them in plastic or freezer wrap. This will help prevent freezer burn.

7. To keep baked goods from drying out, place a piece of bread or an apple in the container with the items. The bread or apple will absorb any excess moisture.

8. If you have a large quantity of baked goods, it is best to freeze them in batches so that you can thaw only what you need for individual servings.

9. If you are sending baked goods to customers, make sure to package them securely with plenty of padding to protect them from damage.

10. If you are baking for an event or special occasion, make sure to allow enough time for baking and cooling before the event. This will give you time to package the items appropriately.

CHAPTER 7: GROWING YOUR BUSINESS. MARKETING AND PROMOTING YOUR ONLINE BAKING BUSINESS

Growing Your online baking Business is an exciting venture that can provide a creative outlet and the potential for a lucrative income. With the rise of online shopping, it can be easier than ever to get your homemade treats out to the world.

Starting an online baking business requires you to have a clear business plan, as well as a deep understanding of food safety, baking and customer service.

STRATEGIES FOR GROWING YOUR ONLINE BAKING BUSINESS

1. Create a Professional Website: First and foremost, create a professional website that showcases your baking products. This will allow potential customers to find you and learn more about your business. Your website should include detailed information about your products, business

policies, payment options, and contact information. **This has been thoroughly discussed already in this book**

2. Develop a Social Media Presence: Social media is an important part of online marketing. Establish a presence on major social media platforms, such as Facebook, Twitter, Instagram, and Pinterest.

Share pictures of your products and engage with potential customers by responding to comments and messages. Create instagram reels, jump on trends and challenges, use trending sounds when making your videos.

Ask your customers to create a review video for you and offer them special discounts for doing that.

Make behind the scene videos, process videos, before and after video, clean up videos and many more to help your customers get to know you better.

3. Offer Discounts and Promotions: Offering discounts and promotions is a great way to attract new customers and retain existing ones. Consider offering discounts for bulk orders, free shipping, or special discounts for first-time customers.

4. Utilize Email Marketing: Email marketing is an effective way to reach customers and promote your business. Develop an email list of potential and existing customers and send them regular emails with updates about your products, discounts, and promotions.

5. Leverage Word-of-Mouth Marketing: Word-of-mouth marketing is one of the most effective marketing strategies. Encourage customers to share their experience with your business and products with friends and family. Offering incentives, such as discount codes or free items, can help encourage customers to spread the word about your business.

6. Focus on Quality: Quality is essential for any business, especially when it comes to baking. Make sure that your products are of the highest quality and that they meet customers' expectations.

7. Create a Loyalty Program: Loyalty programs are a great way to reward loyal customers and encourage them to continue purchasing from your business. Consider offering discounts, free items, or rewards points for repeat customers.

8. Invest in SEO: SEO can help you reach more potential customers and increase sales. Optimize your website and content with relevant keywords and make sure that your website loads quickly.

9. Participate in Local Events: Participating in local events is a great way to get your name out there and meet potential customers. Consider setting up a booth at local festivals or farmers markets.

10. Offer Customized Products: Offering customized products is a great way to stand out from the competition. Allow customers to customize their orders and create unique products that reflect their individual tastes.

11. Expand Your Reach: Consider expanding your reach by offering delivery services to customers in your area. You can also expand your reach by partnering with local businesses to promote your products.

12. Get Creative: Get creative with your online marketing and come up with creative ideas that will help you stand out from the competition. Consider launching a blog or podcast to share your expertise and attract new customers.

TIPS FOR SELLING YOUR PRODUCTS ONLINE

1. Quality Photos: Invest in high-quality photography equipment, or hire a professional photographer, to showcase your product in the best light.

2. Engaging Captions: When it comes to captions, make sure to keep it short and sweet but also engaging. Ask questions and use hashtags to encourage user engagement.

3. Utilize Storytelling: Instagram Stories can be a great way to share behind-the-scenes content and tell a story. Videos that tells stories are a must if you want to stand out with your Content.

4. Cross Promote: Use other social media platforms to promote your product and link back to your Instagram page or website

5. Giveaways: Host giveaways to reward your loyal followers and gain new ones.

6. Use Influencers: Utilize influencers to help promote your product.

7. Run Ads: Consider running paid Instagram ads to reach a wider audience.

8. Track Results: Analyze the results of your posts to determine what is working and what needs to be adjusted.

9. Offer Discounts: Offer discounts or special offers to your followers.

10. Be Consistent: Post regularly and consistently to keep your followers engaged.

11. Be Unique: Any baker who sends out birthday cakes should at least have birthday cards that they would give with heart warming messages for clients.

You can come up with a freebies that the first customer to place an order that day will get a something special. They can get a pick of your next menu or you can offer them an extra gift when next they purchase. Just come up with something unique and exciting.

BUILDING A LOYAL CUSTOMER BASE

Creating a loyal customer base is essential for any business, and starting an online baking business is no exception. Here are some tips to help you build a customer base that sticks around for the long haul.

1. Offer Quality Products: Quality is essential when it comes to baking. Make sure you're using the best ingredients, and that you're following recipes correctly. This will ensure that your customers have a positive experience with your products.

2. Establish Your Brand: Establishing your brand will help you stand out in the online baking space. Develop a unique logo, and create a website that showcases your products and services. You can also use social media to reach potential customers and build brand recognition.

3. Offer Personalized Service: Personalized service is key when it comes to customer loyalty. Make sure customers can easily contact you with any questions or concerns they may have. Additionally, consider offering customer rewards or loyalty programs to reward loyal customers.

4. Be Responsive: Responding quickly and efficiently to customer inquiries is essential for customer loyalty. Make sure you have a customer service system in place that allows you to quickly respond to customer inquiries and

resolve any issues. Employ a staff to help you handle inquiries if you can't do it all on your own.

5. Give Back: Giving back to your community is a great way to build customer loyalty. Consider donating your products to local charities, or offering discounts to customers who use your products to support a good cause.

By implementing these tips, you can build a loyal customer base that will keep coming back for your delicious baked goods. With a bit of effort, you can establish an online baking business that sees success for years to come.

EXPANDING YOUR SERVICES

Expanding your online baking business can be a great way to increase your customer base, improve your profits, and reach a wider audience. Here are some tips for expanding your services:

1. Offer Customization: Give your customers the option to customize their order by adding special ingredients or decorations. This will help them create a unique product that is tailored to their needs and preferences. Suggest adding a handwritten note if it is a gift.

2. Offer Delivery Services: Consider offering delivery services for your customers. This will save them time and make it easier for them to receive their orders. Be sure to check local laws to ensure you are compliant with any regulations regarding food delivery.

3. Add New Products: Expand your product offerings by adding new items to your menu. This will give customers more options to choose from and may encourage them to purchase more from your business. Launch new products at a fair to get your customers excited in anticipation

4. Partner with Local Businesses: Partner with local businesses to offer your products in their stores. This will increase your visibility and help you reach a larger audience.

Also collaborate with other online vendors to create special packages together for Valentines day or a big Holiday. This would also help increase your reach and increase publicity of your brand.

5. Use Social Media: Take advantage of social media to promote your business and reach a wider audience. Use platforms like Facebook, Instagram, Tictok and Twitter to

share photos of your products, post updates about new products, and interact with potential customers.

6. Creating an Email List: Creating an email list is a great way to start an online baking business. An email list is a powerful marketing tool that can help you to reach out to potential customers, build relationships with existing customers, and promote your business.

To create an email list, you will first need to set up that website or blog. This will allow you to capture visitor information such as their name and email address. You can then use this information to add them to your email list.

Once you have built your email list, you can start building relationships with your subscribers by sending them emails with helpful baking tips, recipes, and offers. You can also use your list to send out promotional emails about your business, letting subscribers know about any new products or services you offer.

Creating an email list is essential for growing your online baking business. With an email list, you can build relationships with customers, reach out to potential customers, and promote your business. With the right strategy, you can turn your email list into a powerful marketing tool.

CHAPTER 8. FINAL TIPS FOR SUCCESS

1. Have a Clear Vision for Your Baking Business: Make sure you have a clear vision for your business and establish goals that are realistic and achievable. Focus on creating a long-term plan for success and create a timeline for each goal.

2. Develop a Comprehensive Business Plan: A business plan is an essential tool for any business, and a baking business is no exception. A good business plan will include a description of the products and services you offer, a marketing plan, financial projections and a timeline for achieving your goals.

3. Invest in Quality Equipment: Investing in quality baking equipment is essential to the success of your baking business. Choose the right equipment for the type of baking you plan to do and make sure to research reliable brands.

4. Create an Online Presence: Building an online presence is essential for any small business. Create a website, start a blog and use social media to build an audience.

5. Monitor Your Progress: Track your progress so you can identify areas that need improvement. Use analytics tools to measure website traffic, sales and customer feedback.

6. Stay Up to Date on Industry Trends: Make sure you stay up to date on industry trends and incorporate them into your business. Follow baking blogs, attend baking trade shows and join baking-related professional organizations.

7. Hire an Accountant: Consider hiring an accountant or bookkeeper to help you manage your finances. An accountant can help you with tax preparation, budgeting and financial reporting.

8. Stay Organized: Organization is key to running a successful baking business. Create a filing system to keep track of customer orders and invoices and use scheduling software to help manage your time and resources.

9. Network with Other Bakers: Networking with other bakers is a great way to stay up to date on industry trends, discover new recipes and get advice from experienced

professionals. Join baking forums and attend industry events to connect with other bakers.

10. Have Fun: Running a baking business should be enjoyable. So catch your breath, have fun and take time to relax!

A. STAYING ORGANIZED

Staying organized is essential to running a successful online baking business. Here are some tips to help you get started:

1. **Create a Schedule**: Establish a regular schedule for baking orders and keep it updated. Be sure to include any extra tasks such as shopping for supplies and packaging finished products.

2. **Streamline Your Process**: Develop a system for making your baking process as efficient as possible. This can include pre-measuring ingredients, setting up a dedicated baking space, and labeling your equipment.

3. Track Orders: Maintain a calendar or spreadsheet to track customer orders. This will help you manage orders and keep up with deadlines.

4. Keep Records: Store all of your recipes in one place and keep accurate records of your expenses and income.

5. Stay Connected: Create a website and social media accounts for your business. This can help you attract new customers and keep existing customers informed.

B. PROVIDING EXCELLENT CUSTOMER SERVICE

Providing excellent customer service is essential for any successful online baking business. As the owner of an online baking business, it is important to create a positive customer experience from the start of the purchase process to the delivery of the product.

For example, you could create a FAQ page on your website that answers common customer questions about your products and shipping policies.

You could also offer friendly and timely customer service via phone or online chat. Additionally, you should make sure to keep customers updated throughout the entire purchase process, such as sending out an email when the order is placed, shipped, and delivered.

Finally, make sure that your products are delivered in a timely manner, and that they are of high quality. If a customer is not satisfied with the product, you should offer a refund or a replacement.

This will help ensure that customers are happy with their purchases and will be more likely to come back and purchase more in the future.

Providing excellent customer service is an essential part of running a successful online baking business. Here are some tips for delivering top-notch service:

1. Respond Quickly: Customers want to know that their inquiries and orders are being taken seriously. Reply to customer emails and phone calls promptly, preferably

within 24 hours. If a customer has a special request, do your best to accommodate them.

2. Be Helpful: Offer helpful advice and suggestions to customers. Provide detailed information about the products and services you are offering.

3. Be Clear and Concise: Make sure your communication is clear and concise. Avoid using too many technical terms and jargon.

4. Follow Up: Follow up with customers to ensure they are satisfied with your products and services. Ask them to provide feedback and suggestions on how you can improve your services.

5. Offer Flexible Payment Options: Offer multiple payment options to ensure customers have the flexibility to pay for your products and services in the way that works best for them.

6. Keep Promises: If you promise to deliver something to a customer, make sure you follow through. Failing to keep your promises will damage your reputation and may lead to customer dissatisfaction.

CHAPTER 9. CONCLUSION

In conclusion, starting an online baking business can be a great way to turn your passion into something that can generate income.

Through this guide, you have learned the basics of setting up your online baking business and the steps that you need to take to ensure its success. With the right attitude, patience and hard work, you can become a successful online baker and make your dreams a reality.

So what are you waiting for? Get out there, start baking and make your online baking business a reality!

A SUMMARY OF WHAT YOU'VE LEARNED

The book A Beginner's Guide to Starting an Online Baking Business provided an overview of the essential steps to launching a successful online baking business. The book covered topics such as choosing a business model, setting up an online store, marketing, pricing, and managing finances.

Additionally, the book provided tips on how to improve customer service, build relationships with suppliers, and manage employees. The book concluded with a reminder to entrepreneurs to stay organized, stay focused, and be persistent in the pursuit of their dreams.

Through this book, readers learned that launching an online baking business is a complex process, but with the right knowledge and dedication, it can be achieved.

MOVING FORWARD WITH YOUR ONLINE BAKING BUSINESS

Congratulations on taking the first steps in starting your online baking business! You now have the knowledge and resources to create an effective business plan, build an online presence, and market your business.

With a little bit of hard work and dedication, you can make your online baking business a success. No matter what challenges you face, don't forget to keep moving forward.

With the right attitude and strategy, you can create a thriving baking business that will bring you and your customers joy for many years to come.

FREE STOCK IMAGES

BONUS AND EXTRAS

FOOD PHOTOGRAPHY TIPS

1. Use Natural Lighting: Natural lighting is the most important factor when it comes to taking great photos of baked goods.

Natural light provides a softer, more even lighting than artificial lighting, giving your photos a beautiful warm glow. Try shooting during the early morning or late afternoon hours when the light is softer and warmer.

If you don't have access to natural light, use a tripod and set up your camera to capture the best light available.

2. Invest in Good Equipment: Investing in good quality equipment such as a DSLR camera, lens, and tripod will make a huge difference in the quality of your photos.

A DSLR camera allows you to adjust settings to get the best possible image, and a good lens will help you capture the detail and texture of your baked goods. A tripod will help keep your photos steady and will allow you to take photos from different angles.

3. Use a Macro Lens: A macro lens allows you to capture the intricate details of your baked goods. When photographing small items such as cookies or cupcakes, a macro lens will help you capture the texture and shape of the item.

4. Use Props: Props can help add visual interest to your photos. Try using colorful plates, linens, and utensils to add a pop of color. You can also use ingredients, such as flour and sugar, to add texture and interest.

5. Set the Scene: To create a more dynamic photo, try setting the scene with a few items. This can be as simple as a cutting board or a baking tray. You can also add some fresh flowers or herbs to give the photo a more natural feel.

6. Use High Quality Ingredients: The quality of the ingredients you use will show in the photos. If you are using processed ingredients, take the time to find the best quality you can. This will help your photos look more appetizing.

7. Focus on the Details: Take the time to capture the details of the baked goods. This could be the texture of the crust, the shape of the cookie, or the icing on a cupcake.

Focus on the details and make sure to capture them in the photo.

8. Use a Neutral Background: When photographing baked goods, it's important to use a neutral background. This will help the food stand out in the photo and will also help create a more professional look. You can use a plain white background or a natural texture such as wood or marble.

9. Take Multiple Shots: Take multiple shots of the same item from different angles. This will give you more options to work with and will help ensure you get the perfect photo.

10. Experiment: Don't be afraid to experiment with different angles, lighting, and props. Taking the time to experiment will help you get creative and find new and interesting ways to photograph your baked goods.

These are just a few tips and practical suggestions to help you take better photos of your baked goods. With a little practice and experimentation, you'll soon be producing amazing photos that will make your baked goods look irresistible.

10 EXCLUSIVE RECIPES

1. Caramel Drizzled Apple Pie

Ingredients:

- 2 store-bought refrigerated pie crusts

- 6 apples, peeled, cored and sliced

- 2/3 cup light brown sugar

- 2 tablespoons all-purpose flour

- 1 teaspoon ground cinnamon

- 1/8 teaspoon ground nutmeg

- 2 tablespoons butter

- 1/2 cup granulated sugar

- 1/2 cup packed light brown sugar

- 1/4 cup butter

- 2 tablespoons heavy cream

- 1 teaspoon vanilla extract

Process:

Preheat oven to 375°F.

Place one of the pie crusts in a 9-inch pie plate.

In a large bowl, combine apples, 2/3 cup brown sugar, flour, cinnamon, nutmeg, and 2 tablespoons butter. Toss to coat apples, then spoon into the pie shell. Place the second pie crust on top and pinch the edges together to seal. Cut several small slits in the top for steam to escape.

Bake for 40 minutes or until the top is golden brown.

Meanwhile, in a small saucepan, melt 1/2 cup granulated sugar, 1/2 cup brown sugar, 1/4 cup butter and 2 tablespoons heavy cream over medium heat. Stir until the sugar is dissolved, then bring to a boil. Boil for 3 minutes, stirring constantly. Remove from heat and stir in 1 teaspoon vanilla.

Once the pie is done baking, pour the caramel over the top and let cool before serving.

Prep Time: 15 minutes

Cook Time: 40 minutes

Total Time: 55 minutes

2. FRENCH CHOCOLATE CAKE

Ingredients:

- 2 cups all-purpose flour

- 2 teaspoons baking powder

- 1/2 teaspoon salt

- 1/2 cup butter, softened

- 1 cup granulated sugar

- 2 eggs

- 1 teaspoon vanilla extract

- 1 cup milk

- 1 cup semi-sweet chocolate chips

- 1/2 cup heavy cream

- 1/2 cup powdered sugar

Process:

Preheat oven to 350°F. Grease and flour a 9-inch round cake pan.

In a medium bowl, whisk together flour, baking powder and salt. Set aside.

In a large bowl, cream together butter and sugar until light and fluffy. Beat in eggs one at a time, then stir in vanilla. Alternately add the dry ingredients and milk, beginning and ending with the dry ingredients. Stir in chocolate chips.

Pour the batter into the prepared pan and bake for 30 minutes or until a toothpick inserted into the center comes out clean. Let cool in pan for 10 minutes, then turn out onto a rack to cool completely.

To make the frosting, whip the heavy cream and powdered sugar together until stiff peaks form. Spread over the cooled cake.

Prep Time: 20 minutes

Cook Time: 30 minutes

Total Time: 50 minutes

3. BROWNED BUTTER TOFFEE BLONDIES

Ingredients:

- 1/2 cup butter

- 1 1/4 cups light brown sugar

- 2 eggs

- 1 teaspoon vanilla extract

- 1 cup all-purpose flour

- 1 teaspoon baking powder

- 1/2 teaspoon salt

- 1/2 cup toffee bits

Process:

Preheat oven to 350°F. Grease an 8-inch square baking pan.

In a medium saucepan, melt the butter over medium heat. Cook, stirring occasionally, until the butter is browned and has a nutty aroma. Remove from heat and let cool slightly.

In a large bowl, whisk together brown sugar, eggs and vanilla. Stir in the cooled butter.

In a separate bowl, whisk together flour, baking powder and salt. Gradually stir the dry ingredients into the wet ingredients until just combined. Fold in toffee bits.

Spread the batter into the prepared pan and bake for 25-30 minutes or until a toothpick inserted into the center comes out clean. Let cool in pan before cutting into bars.

Prep Time: 15 minutes

Cook Time: 25-30 minutes

Total Time: 40-45 minutes

4. COCONUT LIME CUPCAKES

Ingredients:

- 2 cups all-purpose flour

- 1 teaspoon baking powder

- 1/2 teaspoon baking soda

- 1/2 teaspoon salt

- 1/2 cup butter, softened

- 1 1/2 cups granulated sugar

- 2 eggs

- 1 teaspoon vanilla extract

- 3/4 cup canned coconut milk

- 1/2 cup shredded coconut

- 1/4 cup lime juice

Process:

Preheat oven to 350°F. Line a 12-cup muffin tin with paper liners. In a medium bowl, whisk together flour, baking powder, baking soda and salt. Set aside.

In a large bowl, cream together butter and sugar until light and fluffy. Beat in eggs one at a time, then stir in vanilla. Alternately add the dry ingredients and coconut milk, beginning and ending with the dry ingredients. Stir in shredded coconut and lime juice.

Fill the muffin cups about 2/3 full and bake for 20-25 minutes or until a toothpick inserted into the center comes out clean. Let cool in the pan for 5 minutes before transferring to a wire rack to cool completely.

Prep Time: 15 minutes

Cook Time: 20-25 minutes

Total Time: 35-40 minutes

5. LEMON LAYER CAKE

Ingredients:

- 2 1/2 cups all-purpose flour

- 2 teaspoons baking powder

- 1/2 teaspoon baking soda

- 1/2 teaspoon salt

- 1 cup butter, softened

- 2 cups granulated sugar

- 4 eggs

- 2 teaspoons vanilla extract

- 1 cup buttermilk

- 2 tablespoons lemon juice

- Zest of 1 lemon

- 2 tablespoons butter, melted

- 2 tablespoons granulated sugar

- 2 tablespoons lemon juice

Process:

Preheat oven to 350°F. Grease and flour two 8-inch round cake pans.

In a medium bowl, whisk together flour, baking powder, baking soda and salt. Set aside.

In a large bowl, cream together butter and sugar until light and fluffy.

Beat in eggs one at a time, then stir in vanilla.

Alternately add the dry ingredients and buttermilk, beginning and ending with the dry ingredients.

Stir in lemon juice and zest.

Divide the batter between the prepared pans and bake for 25-30 minutes or until a toothpick inserted into the center comes out clean.

Let cool in the pans for 10 minutes before turning out onto a wire rack to cool completely.

To make the glaze, whisk together melted butter, sugar and lemon juice.

Drizzle over the cooled cakes.

Prep Time: 15 minutes

Cook Time: 25-30 minutes

Total Time: 40-45 minutes

6. FLOURLESS CHOCOLATE CAKE

Ingredients:

- 2/3 cup butter

- 2 cups semi-sweet chocolate chips

- 1/2 teaspoon salt

- 4 eggs

- 1 cup granulated sugar

- 1 teaspoon vanilla extract

- 1/2 cup chopped walnuts (optional)

Process:

Preheat oven to 350°F.

Grease and flour a 9-inch spring form pan.

In a medium saucepan, melt butter and chocolate chips over low heat. Stir until smooth.

Remove from heat and stir in salt.

In a large bowl, whisk together eggs, sugar and vanilla until light and fluffy.

Gradually stir in the chocolate mixture.

Fold in walnuts, if using.

Pour the batter into the prepared pan and bake for 30-35 minutes or until a toothpick inserted into the center comes out clean.

Let cool in the pan for 10 minutes before turning out onto a wire rack to cool completely.

Prep Time: 10 minutes

Cook Time: 30-35 minutes

Total Time: 40-45 minutes

7. CHOCOLATE CHIP COOKIES

Ingredients:

- 2 1/4 cups all-purpose flour

- 1 teaspoon baking soda

- 1 teaspoon salt

- 1 cup butter, softened

- 3/4 cup granulated sugar

- 3/4 cup packed light brown sugar

- 1 teaspoon vanilla extract

- 2 eggs

- 2 cups semi-sweet chocolate chips

Process:

Preheat oven to 375°F.

Line a baking sheet with parchment paper.

In a medium bowl, whisk together flour, baking soda and salt. Set aside.

In a large bowl, cream together butter and sugars until light and fluffy.

Beat in eggs one at a time, then stir in vanilla.

Gradually stir in the dry ingredients. Fold in chocolate chips.

Drop by tablespoonfuls onto the prepared baking sheet and bake for 8-10 minutes or until golden brown.

Let cool on the baking sheet for 5 minutes before transferring to a wire rack to cool completely.

Prep Time: 15 minutes

Cook Time: 8-10 minutes

Total Time: 23-25 minutes

8. CHOCOLATE HAZELNUT TART

Ingredients:

- 1 store-bought refrigerated pie crust

- 3/4 cup hazelnut spread

- 1 cup semi-sweet chocolate chips

- 1/4 cup heavy cream

- 2 tablespoons butter

- 2 tablespoons light corn syrup

FREE STOCK IMAGES USED

Process:

Preheat oven to 350°F.

Place the pie crust in a 9-inch tart pan and prick the bottom several times with a fork.

Bake for 10-15 minutes or until lightly golden. Let cool.

In a medium bowl, combine hazelnut spread and chocolate chips.

In a small saucepan, heat cream, butter and corn syrup over low heat.

Stir until the butter and chocolate chips are melted and the mixture is smooth.

Pour over the hazelnut spread and stir until combined.

Spread the mixture into the cooled tart shell and refrigerate for at least 2 hours before serving.

Prep Time: 10 minutes

Cook Time: 15 minutes

Total Time: 25 minutes

9. RED VELVET CUPCAKES

Ingredients:

- 2 1/2 cups all-purpose flour

- 2 tablespoons cocoa powder

- 1 teaspoon baking soda

- 1/2 teaspoon salt

- 1 cup butter, softened

- 1 1/2 cups granulated sugar

- 2 eggs

- 1 teaspoon vanilla extract

- 1 cup buttermilk

- 2 tablespoons red food coloring

- 1 teaspoon white vinegar

Process:

Preheat oven to 350°F.

Line a 12-cup muffin tin with paper liners.

In a medium bowl, whisk together flour, cocoa powder, baking soda and salt. Set aside.

In a large bowl, cream together butter and sugar until light and fluffy.

Beat in eggs one at a time, then stir in vanilla.

Alternately add the dry ingredients and buttermilk, beginning and ending with the dry ingredients.

Stir in food coloring and vinegar.

Fill the muffin cups about 2/3 full and bake for 20-25 minutes or until a toothpick inserted into the center comes out clean.

Let cool in the pan for 5 minutes before transferring to a wire rack to cool completely.

Prep Time: 15 minutes

Cook Time: 20-25 minutes

Total Time: 35-40 minutes

10. PEANUT BUTTER BROWNIES

Ingredients:

- 1/2 cup butter

- 1 cup semi-sweet chocolate chips

- 3/4 cup light brown sugar

- 1 teaspoon vanilla extract

- 2 eggs

- 1/2 cup all-purpose flour

- 1/2 teaspoon baking powder

-1/4 teaspoon salt

-1/2cup creamy peanut butter

Process:

Preheat oven to 350°F.

Grease an 8-inch square baking pan.

In a medium saucepan, melt butter and chocolate chips over low heat.

Stir until smooth.

Remove from heat and stir in brown sugar, vanilla and eggs.

In a small bowl, whisk together flour, baking powder and salt.

Gradually stir the dry ingredients into the wet ingredients until just combined.

Spread half of the batter into the prepared pan.

Drop spoonfuls of peanut butter over the batter and spread evenly.

Spread the remaining batter over the peanut butter.

Bake for 25-30 minutes or until a toothpick inserted into the center comes out clean. Let cool in pan before cutting into bars.

Prep Time: 15 minutes

Cook Time: 25-30 minutes

Total Time: 40-45 minutes

SEASONED ADVICE FROM EXPERIENCED BAKERS

1. "Always Have a Plan" - Susan Smith, Professional Pastry Chef.

2. "Measure Twice, Bake Once" - John Doe, Experienced Home Baker.

3. "Know Your Ingredients" - Jane Smith, Professional Bread Baker.

4. "Baking is Science, Not Magic" - Joe Brown, Master Baker.

5. "Be Patient and Have Fun" - Larry White, Experienced Cake Decorator.

6. Jack Brown: A professional baker with 20 years of experience, Jack Brown recommends thoroughly measuring all ingredients ahead of time, as mismeasured ingredients can ruin the final outcome of a bake.

7. Maria Gomez: With 15 years of baking experience, Maria Gomez stresses the importance of preheating the oven before baking. A cold oven can lead to uneven baking, resulting in an unappetizing final product.

8. Tom Watson: A pastry chef with over 10 years of experience, Tom Watson shares the importance of double-checking recipes. Even a small change in a recipe can drastically alter the end product.

9. Sarah Johnson: With a passion for cake decorating, Sarah Johnson suggests using high-quality ingredients for a superior result. She recommends looking for organic, sustainably sourced ingredients whenever possible.

10. Alex Smith: An experienced baker and cake designer, Alex Smith advises to be patient and trust the process. Baking can be a test of patience, but with patience and care, the end result is always worth it.

ADVICE WITH REGARDS RUNNING AN ONLINE BAKERY

1. Don't be afraid to try new things. - Jenni from Jenni's Baked Goods

Jenni has been running her online baking business for two years. She has found success by experimenting with different flavors and recipes, and has seen her business grow as a result.

2. Quality is key. - Alex from Sweet Treats Bakery

Alex has been in the baking industry for over ten years and has seen how important quality is in winning customers over. He always recommends his customers try out his goodies and he knows that they will come back if they are satisfied.

3. Have a plan and stick to it. - Amber from Amber's Sweet Shop

Amber has been running her online bakery for four years now. She has found that having a plan and sticking to it is the key to success. She also recommends setting goals and tracking progress to ensure that you are always on the right track.

4. Connect with your customers. - John from John's Bakery

John has been in the baking industry for almost 20 years and knows how important it is to keep in touch with customers. He recommends connecting with customers on social media and offering discounts to those who follow and share his business.

5. Keep learning. - Matt from Matt's Cakes

Matt has been baking cakes since he was a kid. He recommends that any baker looking to succeed should never stop learning new techniques and recipes. He also stresses the importance of keeping up with new trends in the industry.

6. Focus on customer service. - Lara from Lara's Baking Company

Lara has been running her online baking business for five years now. She has found that customer service is paramount in any business, and she always ensures her customers are satisfied with their orders.

7. Don't be afraid to be creative. - Steve from Steve's Baked Goods

Steve has been working in the baking industry for nearly 15 years. He recommends that bakers don't be afraid to try new things and be creative when it comes to their recipes and products.

8. Network with other bakers. - Sarah from Sarah's Cakes

Sarah has been in the baking industry for over eight years and knows how important it is to network with other bakers in the industry. She recommends attending conferences and other events to network and learn from other experienced bakers.

9. Invest in quality ingredients. - Anna from Anna's Patisserie

Anna has been a baker for seven years and she knows that quality ingredients are essential for a successful baking business. She recommends investing in quality ingredients to ensure that customers can always enjoy the best product.

10. Have a strong online presence. - Tom from Tom's Bakery

Tom has been running his online bakery for three years now. He has found that having a strong online presence is key to success. He recommends having a website, social media accounts and a blog to help promote your business.

NOTE: Some names have been changed for privacy reasons

THE END

ACTION PLAN

ACTION PLAN

ACTION PLAN

ACTION PLAN

ACTION PLAN

ACTION PLAN

ACTON PLAN